PRINCEWILL LAGANG

Green Entrepreneurship: Sustainable Business for a Changing World

Contents

1

Green Entrepreneurship: Sustainable Business for a Changing World

Introduction

In a rapidly changing world, where environmental concerns, resource depletion, and climate change are at the forefront of global discussions, a new breed of entrepreneurs is emerging. These individuals are not just motivated by profit but by a deep-seated commitment to environmental sustainability and social responsibility. This first chapter sets the stage for our exploration of green entrepreneurship, focusing on the context, motivations, and the pressing need for sustainable business practices in today's world.

Section 1: The Changing Landscape

1.1 The Environmental Imperative

The opening section highlights the ever-growing environmental challenges our planet faces. It discusses climate change, biodiversity loss, resource scarcity, and pollution as critical issues that demand our attention. Real-life examples and statistics underscore the urgency of addressing these problems.

1.2 The Role of Business

This section explores the significant role that businesses play in contributing to environmental degradation but also how they can be part of the solution. It discusses the concept of the "triple bottom line," emphasizing that businesses should consider not only profits but also the social and environmental impacts of their operations.

Section 2: The Rise of Green Entrepreneurship

2.1 Defining Green Entrepreneurship

Here, we provide a comprehensive definition of green entrepreneurship, highlighting its distinct characteristics and its overarching goal to create environmentally and socially responsible businesses. We discuss how this concept goes beyond traditional entrepreneurship and necessitates a holistic approach to addressing sustainability challenges.

2.2 Motivations and Drivers

This section delves into the motivations that drive individuals to become green entrepreneurs. We examine factors such as personal values, ethical considerations, market opportunities, and the desire to make a positive impact. Interviews with successful green entrepreneurs provide insights into what inspires their work.

Section 3: The Green Entrepreneurial Ecosystem

3.1 The Supportive Infrastructure

This part explores the various elements that make up the ecosystem for green entrepreneurs. It includes government policies, financial incentives, incubators, accelerators, and organizations dedicated to sustainability. We emphasize how these support structures are crucial in nurturing and scaling green businesses.

3.2 Challenges and Obstacles

Every entrepreneurial journey comes with its share of challenges. In this section, we discuss the unique obstacles green entrepreneurs encounter, including capital constraints, market skepticism, and regulatory hurdles. Strategies for overcoming these challenges are also explored.

Section 4: Case Studies

4.1 Success Stories

The chapter provides several case studies of successful green entrepreneurs and their businesses. These examples showcase the diverse range of industries and business models within green entrepreneurship. We explore their journeys, innovations, and the positive impact they have had on the environment and society.

4.2 Lessons Learned

From the case studies, we extract valuable lessons that aspiring green entrepreneurs can apply to their own ventures. These include insights into sustainable business models, effective marketing strategies, and how to navigate the complexities of the green economy.

Conclusion

Chapter 1 concludes by emphasizing the timeliness and importance of green entrepreneurship in a changing world. It reiterates the interconnectedness of environmental and economic well-being, highlighting the potential for positive change through sustainable business practices. It sets the stage for the subsequent chapters, where we will delve deeper into the strategies, skills, and tools required for aspiring green entrepreneurs to make a meaningful impact.

2

Understanding Sustainability in Green Entrepreneurship

Introduction

In the previous chapter, we introduced the concept of green entrepreneurship and its significance in addressing environmental and social challenges. In Chapter 2, we will explore the foundational principles of sustainability that underpin green entrepreneurship. Understanding sustainability is critical for aspiring green entrepreneurs as it forms the basis for designing and operating environmentally and socially responsible businesses.

Section 1: Defining Sustainability

1.1 The Three Pillars of Sustainability

This section provides a comprehensive definition of sustainability, emphasizing the three interconnected pillars: economic, environmental, and social. We discuss how these pillars are interdependent and how green entrepreneurs must balance them to create lasting impact.

1.2 The Sustainable Development Goals (SDGs)

We delve into the United Nations' Sustainable Development Goals and how they serve as a global roadmap for addressing pressing environmental and social issues. We highlight the role green entrepreneurs play in contributing to the achievement of these goals.

Section 2: Sustainable Business Models

2.1 Cradle to Cradle: A New Paradigm

We introduce the "Cradle to Cradle" (C2C) framework, emphasizing a regenerative approach to business. C2C aims to eliminate waste and pollution while promoting the continual reuse of resources. This section discusses how green entrepreneurs can adopt C2C principles in their ventures.

2.2 Circular Economy

Exploring the circular economy concept, we discuss the importance of resource efficiency and how green entrepreneurs can design their businesses to minimize waste and maximize the value of materials. Real-world examples of companies successfully implementing circular economy principles are showcased.

Section 3: Metrics and Measurement

3.1 Environmental Impact Assessment

This section explores various methods and tools for measuring the environmental impact of businesses, such as life cycle assessment (LCA) and carbon footprint analysis. We emphasize the importance of quantifying and managing environmental impacts to improve sustainability.

3.2 Social Impact Assessment

Green entrepreneurs are encouraged to assess their social impact through metrics like social return on investment (SROI). We discuss the challenges of quantifying social impact and provide guidance on gathering relevant data.

Section 4: Legal and Ethical Considerations

4.1 Regulatory Compliance

We examine the legal aspects of green entrepreneurship, including environmental regulations, certifications, and standards. Understanding and complying with these legal requirements is crucial for avoiding pitfalls and ensuring the sustainability of the business.

4.2 Ethical Practices

The section delves into the ethical considerations that green entrepreneurs should keep in mind, including fair labor practices, supply chain ethics, and responsible marketing. We discuss how transparency and ethical behavior can build trust with customers and partners.

Conclusion

Chapter 2 concludes by emphasizing the foundational role of sustainability in green entrepreneurship. It underscores the need for aspiring green entrepreneurs to integrate sustainability principles into their business models, operations, and decision-making processes. Understanding sustainability and its various facets is essential for creating businesses that not only generate profits but also make a positive impact on the environment and society. Chapter 3 will build upon these principles, exploring the practical steps involved in launching and scaling a green venture.

3

Launching Your Green Entrepreneurial Venture

Introduction

Having established the foundational principles of green entrepreneurship and sustainability in the previous chapters, Chapter 3 provides a practical roadmap for aspiring green entrepreneurs to launch their sustainable ventures. This chapter guides you through the steps, strategies, and considerations for starting a green business and bringing your vision to life.

Section 1: Identifying Your Green Business Idea

1.1 Passion and Purpose

We begin with the importance of identifying a business idea that aligns with your personal values and passion for sustainability. We discuss how a genuine commitment to making a positive environmental and social impact can drive your business forward.

1.2 Market Research

This section explores the significance of market research in identifying niche opportunities and gauging demand for your green product or service. We delve into methods for conducting effective market research within the context of green entrepreneurship.

Section 2: Business Planning and Strategy

2.1 Business Model Canvas

We introduce the Business Model Canvas as a tool for outlining the key components of your business, including your value proposition, customer segments, revenue streams, and distribution channels. We emphasize the need for aligning your business model with sustainability principles.

2.2 Sustainability Strategy

This section guides you in formulating a sustainability strategy for your venture. It covers aspects such as resource efficiency, ethical sourcing, and minimizing environmental impact while maximizing social benefit.

Section 3: Funding Your Green Venture

3.1 Financing Options

We explore various financing options available to green entrepreneurs, including bootstrapping, seeking investors, applying for grants, and crowdfunding. Understanding these options is crucial for securing the necessary resources to get your business off the ground.

3.2 Impact Investment

This section delves into the growing field of impact investment, where investors support businesses that aim to generate both financial returns and positive social and environmental outcomes. We discuss how to attract impact investors who align with your sustainability goals.

Section 4: Legal and Regulatory Compliance

4.1 Business Structure

Choosing the right legal structure for your green business is crucial. We discuss the pros and cons of different structures, such as sole proprietorship, LLC, or B Corp, and how they impact your ability to integrate sustainability into your operations.

4.2 Permits and Certifications

Navigating the regulatory landscape is essential for green entrepreneurs. We cover the permits, certifications, and compliance requirements specific to green businesses, helping you stay on the right side of the law.

Section 5: Marketing and Branding

5.1 Green Marketing Strategies

This section explores marketing strategies tailored to green businesses. We discuss how to effectively communicate your sustainability message to eco-conscious consumers and build a loyal customer base.

5.2 Building a Sustainable Brand

Creating a strong and authentic brand is essential for success. We provide guidance on crafting a brand identity that reflects your commitment to sustainability, ethical practices, and your unique value proposition.

Conclusion

Chapter 3 concludes by emphasizing the importance of careful planning and a strong commitment to sustainability in launching a green entrepreneurial venture. By following the steps and strategies outlined in this chapter, aspiring green entrepreneurs can lay the foundation for a business that not only generates profits but also contributes positively to the environment and society. Chapter 4 will focus on the crucial aspects of scaling and growing your green business once it's up and running.

4

Scaling and Growing Your Green Business

Introduction

In Chapter 3, we discussed how to launch a green entrepreneurial venture, emphasizing the importance of sustainability, passion, and careful planning. In Chapter 4, we shift our focus to the critical phase of scaling and growing your green business. This chapter provides insights, strategies, and considerations for expanding your impact, reaching a wider audience, and making your sustainable business thrive.

Section 1: Expanding Your Product or Service Offerings

1.1 Diversification

We explore the concept of diversification in the context of green entrepreneurship. This section discusses the benefits of offering a range of sustainable products or services that cater to different market segments and can contribute to a more stable revenue stream.

1.2 Product Innovation

Innovation is a key driver of growth. We delve into the importance of continually improving and innovating your offerings to stay relevant in a rapidly changing market. Case studies of successful green product innovation are included.

Section 2: Marketing and Branding for Growth

2.1 Digital Marketing Strategies

In the digital age, effective online marketing is essential for expanding your reach. This section discusses digital marketing strategies, including social media, content marketing, and online advertising, with a focus on sustainability messaging.

2.2 Storytelling and Brand Narrative

We explore the power of storytelling in green entrepreneurship. Crafting a compelling narrative around your brand and sustainability efforts can resonate with consumers and differentiate your business in a competitive market.

Section 3: Expanding Distribution and Reach

3.1 E-commerce and Online Sales

In an increasingly connected world, e-commerce plays a vital role in reaching a broader audience. We discuss the strategies and tools for successfully selling your green products or services online.

3.2 Partnerships and Collaborations

Forming strategic partnerships with like-minded organizations can be a powerful way to expand your reach. This section covers how to identify and leverage partnerships for mutual benefit and increased impact.

Section 4: Financing Growth

4.1 Scaling Capital

Scaling your green business often requires additional capital. We explore different sources of financing for growth, including venture capital, loans, and revenue reinvestment.

4.2 Impact Investment

Building on the concept introduced in Chapter 3, we discuss how to attract impact investors who share your commitment to sustainability and are willing to support your business's growth.

Section 5: Managing Sustainability at Scale

5.1 Supply Chain Management

As your business grows, managing a sustainable supply chain becomes increasingly important. We explore strategies for ensuring the ethical sourcing of materials and reducing the environmental footprint of your operations.

5.2 Reporting and Transparency

Transparency and reporting are critical for maintaining trust with customers and investors. We discuss sustainability reporting frameworks and the importance of disclosing your environmental and social impact.

Conclusion

Chapter 4 concludes by highlighting the significance of scaling and growing your green business to maximize your positive environmental and social impact. By implementing the strategies and considerations outlined in this chapter, you can work toward creating a successful, sustainable business that not only thrives but also contributes meaningfully to a changing world. Chapter 5 will focus on the challenges and opportunities of sustaining long-term success in green entrepreneurship, emphasizing resilience and adaptability.

5

Sustaining Long-Term Success in Green Entrepreneurship

Introduction

As your green entrepreneurial venture grows and thrives, it faces a unique set of challenges and opportunities. In Chapter 5, we delve into the key factors for sustaining long-term success in green entrepreneurship. This chapter explores strategies for maintaining resilience, adaptability, and a strong commitment to sustainability as your business matures.

Section 1: Resilience and Adaptability

1.1 Building Resilience

We discuss the importance of resilience in navigating the uncertainties of the business world. We explore strategies for building a resilient organization that can weather economic, environmental, and social challenges.

1.2 Adaptability to Change

Adaptability is crucial for long-term success. This section focuses on the ability to pivot, evolve, and embrace change when necessary. We provide examples of businesses that have successfully adapted to remain relevant and sustainable.

Section 2: Innovation and R&D

2.1 Continuous Innovation

Innovation remains a cornerstone of success. We discuss the need for ongoing research and development to stay at the forefront of sustainable technology, practices, and consumer trends.

2.2 Sustainable Innovation

This section explores the concept of sustainable innovation, where businesses create new products, services, and processes that have a positive environmental and social impact. We showcase examples of sustainable innovation in green entrepreneurship.

Section 3: Social Responsibility and Impact

3.1 Community Engagement

Engaging with your local community and broader society is integral to long-term success. We discuss how green entrepreneurs can make a positive impact through community initiatives, partnerships, and social responsibility programs.

3.2 Measuring and Communicating Impact

Continuously measuring and communicating your environmental and social impact is crucial. This section covers the tools and frameworks available for quantifying and disclosing your sustainability achievements.

Section 4: Scaling with Purpose

4.1 Ethical Growth

We emphasize the importance of growth with a clear purpose. Scaling should be aligned with your sustainability goals, ensuring that every expansion contributes positively to the environment and society.

4.2 Global Expansion

For green entrepreneurs looking to expand globally, we provide insights into the challenges and opportunities of international markets, emphasizing the need for cross-cultural sensitivity and adaptation.

Section 5: Leadership and Team Development

5.1 Leadership for Sustainability

Strong leadership is essential for maintaining your organization's commitment to sustainability. We explore the traits and qualities of effective leaders in green entrepreneurship.

5.2 Team Building and Talent Retention

As your business grows, building and retaining a skilled and motivated team becomes increasingly important. We discuss strategies for attracting, developing, and retaining talent in a competitive market.

Conclusion

Chapter 5 concludes by underlining the continuous commitment to sustainability and adaptability as essential elements for sustaining long-term success in green entrepreneurship. By incorporating the strategies and considerations discussed in this chapter, green entrepreneurs can navigate the evolving business landscape while staying true to their mission of creating positive environmental and social impact. Chapter 6 will look ahead to the future of green entrepreneurship and emerging trends in the field.

6

The Future of Green Entrepreneurship: Emerging Trends and Opportunities

Introduction

In this final chapter, we shift our focus to the future of green entrepreneurship. We explore the emerging trends, opportunities, and challenges that green entrepreneurs are likely to encounter in the coming years. Understanding these developments is essential for staying at the forefront of sustainability and innovation.

Section 1: Technological Advancements

1.1 Clean Energy and Renewable Technologies

We discuss the rapid advancements in clean energy sources, such as solar and wind, and their increasing accessibility for green entrepreneurs. We explore opportunities in renewable energy generation and storage.

1.2 Sustainable Transportation

Green entrepreneurs are well-positioned to leverage innovations in sustainable transportation, including electric vehicles, autonomous mobility, and alternative fuels. We delve into the potential for sustainable transportation startups.

Section 2: Circular Economy and Sustainable Materials

2.1 Circular Business Models

The circular economy continues to gain momentum. We explore how green entrepreneurs can capitalize on the growing demand for products and services that minimize waste and promote resource efficiency.

2.2 Biodegradable and Eco-Friendly Materials

With a shift towards sustainable and eco-friendly materials, this section discusses opportunities for green entrepreneurs in the development and use of biodegradable and renewable materials.

Section 3: Health and Wellness

3.1 Green Healthcare

The intersection of sustainability and healthcare is a burgeoning field. We discuss opportunities for green entrepreneurs in areas such as sustainable medical devices, green healthcare facilities, and eco-friendly healthcare products.

3.2 Wellness and Eco-friendly Living

The wellness industry offers numerous opportunities for green entrepreneurs. We explore sustainable alternatives for health and wellness products, as well as the growth of eco-friendly living solutions.

Section 4: Climate Resilience and Adaptation

4.1 Climate-Resilient Infrastructure

As climate change impacts become more pronounced, green entrepreneurs can play a critical role in designing and building climate-resilient infrastructure, including flood-resistant buildings and smart urban planning.

4.2 Eco-Friendly Technologies for Adaptation

This section discusses the potential for green entrepreneurs to develop technologies and solutions that help communities and businesses adapt to the challenges posed by a changing climate.

Section 5: Policy and Regulation

5.1 Environmental Regulations

We explore the evolving landscape of environmental regulations and how they can impact green entrepreneurs. Staying informed and engaged in policy discussions is vital for success.

5.2 Supportive Policies

Green entrepreneurs can benefit from supportive policies, including tax incentives, grants, and subsidies. This section provides insights into navigating the evolving policy environment.

Conclusion

Chapter 6 concludes by emphasizing the dynamic and promising future of green entrepreneurship. As the world continues to grapple with pressing environmental and social challenges, green entrepreneurs have a pivotal role to play in creating innovative, sustainable solutions. By staying informed and adaptable, green entrepreneurs can seize emerging opportunities and remain at the forefront of sustainable business practices. The journey of green entrepreneurship is ongoing, and this chapter serves as a reminder that the commitment to sustainability remains a powerful force for positive change in our rapidly changing world.

7

The Legacy of Green Entrepreneurship and Conclusion

Introduction

In the final chapter of this book, we reflect on the legacy of green entrepreneurship and its profound impact on the business world and the environment. We recap the key takeaways from previous chapters and conclude with a call to action for current and future green entrepreneurs.

Section 1: The Impact of Green Entrepreneurship

1.1 Environmental and Social Change

We discuss the tangible environmental and social changes that green entrepreneurship has brought about. We provide real-world examples of how green businesses have reduced carbon emissions, improved resource efficiency, and advanced social equity.

1.2 Cultural and Consumer Shifts

This section explores how green entrepreneurship has contributed to a cultural shift toward sustainability. It discusses how consumer behaviors and expectations have evolved, driven by conscious consumption and ethical choices.

Section 2: Challenges and Lessons Learned

2.1 Overcoming Challenges

We reflect on the challenges and obstacles green entrepreneurs face on their journey. From funding difficulties to regulatory hurdles, we highlight stories of resilience and determination.

2.2 Valuable Lessons

Green entrepreneurship has provided numerous lessons for aspiring entrepreneurs. We summarize the key takeaways, including the importance of passion, adaptability, and a commitment to sustainability.

Section 3: The Ongoing Mission

3.1 A Pledge for the Future

We underscore the ongoing commitment required in green entrepreneurship. As the environmental and social challenges continue to evolve, we encourage green entrepreneurs to remain steadfast in their mission.

3.2 Expanding the Movement

This section discusses the need to expand the reach and impact of green entrepreneurship. It encourages collaboration, mentorship, and knowledge sharing within the community.

Section 4: The Legacy of Green Entrepreneurs

4.1 Success Stories

We highlight the legacies of prominent green entrepreneurs and their contributions to the field. Their stories inspire and serve as a testament to the enduring impact of green entrepreneurship.

4.2 A Vision for the Future

In closing, we present a vision for the future where green entrepreneurship is not just a niche but a mainstream approach to business. We discuss the potential for sustainable, circular, and regenerative economies.

Conclusion

Chapter 7 concludes by celebrating the legacy of green entrepreneurship and its enduring impact on the world. It serves as a reminder that every green entrepreneur, through their passion and commitment to sustainability, plays a vital role in creating a better future for our planet and its inhabitants. The journey of green entrepreneurship is a continuous one, and it is our hope that this book has provided inspiration and guidance for those who wish to embark on or further their commitment to the path of sustainable and responsible business.

8

Resources and Further Reading

Introduction

In this final chapter, we provide a curated list of resources and further reading materials for green entrepreneurs and individuals interested in sustainability and sustainable business practices. These resources include books, websites, organizations, and tools to help you continue your journey in green entrepreneurship and deepen your understanding of environmental and social responsibility.

Section 1: Recommended Books

1.1 "Cradle to Cradle: Remaking the Way We Make Things" by William McDonough and Michael Braungart
   - This groundbreaking book introduces the concept of the circular economy and how products can be designed for environmental and social benefit.

1.2 "The Lean Startup: How Today's Entrepreneurs Use Continuous Innovation to Create Radically Successful Businesses" by Eric Ries
   - While not specifically focused on green entrepreneurship, this book pro-

vides valuable insights on building a business with efficiency and adaptability.

1.3 "The Upcycle: Beyond Sustainability—Designing for Abundance" by William McDonough and Michael Braungart
  - A follow-up to "Cradle to Cradle," this book explores how we can go beyond sustainability and design for abundance.

Section 2: Online Resources

2.1 GreenBiz (Website: www.greenbiz.com)
  - GreenBiz is a leading source of news, events, and research on sustainable business practices, providing valuable insights and resources for green entrepreneurs.

2.2 B Lab (Website: www.bcorporation.net)
  - B Lab is a non-profit organization that certifies B Corporations (B Corps) and provides resources for businesses aiming to balance profit and purpose.

2.3 Sustainable Brands (Website: www.sustainablebrands.com)
  - Sustainable Brands offers a global community of business innovators who are leading the way to a sustainable future, with articles, events, and resources.

Section 3: Organizations and Associations

3.1 The Green Entrepreneurship Network (Website: www.greenentrepreneurship.org)
  - This global network connects green entrepreneurs, offers resources, and facilitates collaboration in the field of sustainability and entrepreneurship.

3.2 The Sustainable Business Network (Website: www.sbn.co.nz)
  - Operating in New Zealand, the Sustainable Business Network connects and supports businesses seeking to incorporate sustainability into their

operations.

Section 4: Tools and Frameworks

4.1 Global Reporting Initiative (GRI) (Website: www.globalreporting.org)
   - GRI provides a framework for sustainability reporting, offering guidelines and standards to measure and communicate your business's environmental and social impact.

4.2 Life Cycle Assessment (LCA) Tools
   - Various LCA tools are available to assess the environmental impacts of your products or services, including SimaPro and openLCA.

Conclusion

Chapter 8 provides valuable resources and further reading materials to support your journey as a green entrepreneur. Whether you're looking for inspiration, practical tools, or connections within the sustainability community, these resources can help you continue your mission of creating positive environmental and social impact through your business. As the field of green entrepreneurship continues to evolve, staying informed and connected to these resources is essential for your ongoing success and impact.

9

Your Personal Journey in Green Entrepreneurship

Introduction

In this chapter, we shift our focus from external resources to your personal journey as a green entrepreneur. You are the driving force behind your sustainable business, and your mindset, values, and personal development are integral to your success. This chapter explores personal growth, self-care, and the role of ethics and values in your green entrepreneurial journey.

Section 1: Personal Growth and Development

1.1 Lifelong Learning

Green entrepreneurship is a dynamic field, and continuous learning is essential for staying ahead. We discuss the importance of personal development and how it can enhance your skills and decision-making.

1.2 Resilience and Adaptability

As a green entrepreneur, you will face challenges. This section delves into the development of resilience and adaptability to navigate obstacles and maintain a positive outlook.

Section 2: Balancing Passion and Well-being

2.1 Passion for Purpose

We explore the significance of aligning your personal passion with your business's purpose. This alignment can provide motivation and fulfillment, but it's essential to maintain a healthy work-life balance.

2.2 Self-care and Well-being

Running a green business can be demanding. We emphasize the importance of self-care practices to avoid burnout and maintain your mental and physical well-being.

Section 3: Ethics and Values

3.1 The Role of Ethics

Ethical considerations are at the core of green entrepreneurship. We discuss the importance of upholding ethical standards in all business dealings.

3.2 Values-Driven Leadership

As a green entrepreneur, your values influence your business decisions. We explore how values-driven leadership can create a positive impact on your business and the broader community.

Conclusion

Chapter 9 concludes by emphasizing the personal aspects of your journey as a green entrepreneur. Your personal growth, well-being, and values play a crucial role in the success of your sustainable business. By nurturing these elements, you can maintain your commitment to sustainability and create a lasting impact in the field of green entrepreneurship.

10

Fostering a Sustainable Legacy and Continuous Impact

I ntroduction

In this final chapter, we explore the legacy you can leave as a green entrepreneur and how your efforts can continue to have a positive impact on the environment and society. We discuss the importance of long-term thinking, the potential for mentorship, and the role of legacy-building in green entrepreneurship.

Section 1: Long-Term Thinking

1.1 The Power of Long-Term Vision

We emphasize the importance of maintaining a long-term perspective in green entrepreneurship. This approach ensures that your business decisions contribute to lasting positive impacts on the environment and society.

1.2 Strategic Planning

Long-term thinking involves strategic planning. We explore how to set goals, create roadmaps, and adapt your strategies to the evolving challenges and opportunities in the field of sustainability.

Section 2: Mentorship and Knowledge Sharing

2.1 Passing the Torch

Mentoring emerging green entrepreneurs can be a rewarding way to leave a sustainable legacy. We discuss the importance of knowledge sharing and how it can benefit both mentors and mentees.

2.2 Supporting the Next Generation

Green entrepreneurship is a field that will continue to evolve. We explore ways to support and inspire the next generation of eco-conscious entrepreneurs and leaders.

Section 3: Measuring and Communicating Impact

3.1 Impact Assessment

We discuss the importance of ongoing impact assessment, using tools and metrics to measure your business's environmental and social contributions.

3.2 Transparency and Reporting

Communicating your impact is essential for building trust with stakeholders. We explore the various channels and frameworks for transparently sharing your sustainability achievements.

Conclusion

Chapter 10 concludes by highlighting the significance of fostering a sustainable legacy and maintaining a continuous impact in green entrepreneurship. As a green entrepreneur, your journey is not just about building a successful business but leaving a positive mark on the world. By embracing long-term thinking, supporting future generations, and transparently communicating your impact, you can ensure that your legacy endures and contributes to a more sustainable future. Your journey in green entrepreneurship is an ongoing mission, and this chapter serves as a reminder that your dedication to sustainability can create a lasting and meaningful impact.

11

Challenges and Future Considerations in Green Entrepreneurship

I ntroduction

In this chapter, we explore the ongoing and emerging challenges faced by green entrepreneurs and consider the future landscape of green entrepreneurship. Understanding these challenges and trends is vital for sustainability-focused businesses as they navigate a dynamic and evolving environment.

Section 1: Ongoing Challenges

1.1 Economic Uncertainties

Economic fluctuations and uncertainties can impact the funding and growth of green businesses. We discuss strategies for financial stability and resilience in the face of economic challenges.

1.2 Regulatory Landscape

Regulatory requirements and policies related to sustainability and the environment are constantly evolving. Staying compliant and adapting to new regulations can be a significant challenge for green entrepreneurs.

Section 2: Emerging Trends and Opportunities

2.1 Advancements in Technology

We explore how emerging technologies, such as artificial intelligence, blockchain, and data analytics, are opening up new opportunities for green entrepreneurs to enhance their operations and impact.

2.2 Consumer Behavior and Trends

Consumer preferences are shifting toward sustainable and eco-friendly products and services. We discuss how understanding and responding to these changing preferences can drive growth.

Section 3: The Circular Economy

3.1 Circular Business Models

The circular economy is gaining traction as a sustainable alternative to traditional linear production. We delve into how green entrepreneurs can take advantage of circular business models.

3.2 Resource Efficiency and Eco-Design

We explore how resource efficiency and eco-design are integral to the circular economy. Businesses that reduce waste and maximize resource utilization can excel in a circular economy.

Conclusion

Chapter 11 concludes by emphasizing the importance of being prepared for ongoing challenges and seizing emerging opportunities in green entrepreneurship. By understanding the evolving landscape of sustainability, green entrepreneurs can navigate obstacles and continue to thrive in a rapidly changing world. The journey of green entrepreneurship is ongoing, and this chapter serves as a reminder that challenges are part of the path to making a meaningful and lasting impact on the environment and society.

12

The Global Impact of Green Entrepreneurship

Introduction

In this final chapter, we zoom out to examine the broader global impact of green entrepreneurship. We explore how green entrepreneurs contribute to addressing global environmental and social challenges, influence policy, and inspire change. This chapter underscores the significance of green entrepreneurship as a catalyst for positive global transformation.

Section 1: Environmental and Social Impact

1.1 Addressing Global Challenges

Green entrepreneurs are on the frontline of addressing pressing global issues, such as climate change, resource depletion, and social inequality. We discuss how their innovations and sustainable practices play a crucial role in mitigating these challenges.

1.2 Global Reach

We highlight examples of green entrepreneurs whose impact extends beyond their local communities to make a difference on a global scale. From renewable energy projects to eco-friendly products, their work has worldwide implications.

Section 2: Policy and Advocacy

2.1 Influencing Sustainability Policies

Green entrepreneurs often advocate for policies that support sustainability and social responsibility. We explore how their efforts can shape local, national, and international policy decisions.

2.2 The Role of B Corporations

We discuss the B Corporation movement and how certified B Corps are working collectively to redefine success in business and advocate for policy changes that benefit the environment and society.

Section 3: Inspiring Change

3.1 Entrepreneurial Role Models

Green entrepreneurs serve as role models for aspiring entrepreneurs and businesses seeking to incorporate sustainability into their operations. Their successes inspire others to follow a similar path.

3.2 Shifting Cultural Norms

The impact of green entrepreneurship goes beyond the business world. We discuss how these entrepreneurs contribute to shifting cultural norms and expectations around environmental responsibility and ethical business practices.

Conclusion

Chapter 12 concludes by underscoring the global impact of green entrepreneurship. The work of green entrepreneurs is a driving force in addressing critical global challenges, shaping policies, and inspiring change. Their commitment to sustainability and social responsibility serves as a model for businesses worldwide. As the field of green entrepreneurship continues to grow and evolve, it plays an increasingly pivotal role in the global movement toward a more sustainable and equitable future.

Throughout this book, we've embarked on a comprehensive journey into the world of green entrepreneurship, from the foundational principles to its global impact. Here's a brief summary of the key chapters:

1. Introduction and Context: We began by setting the stage, exploring the urgent need for sustainable business practices in our rapidly changing world. Environmental and social challenges provide the backdrop for green entrepreneurship.

2. Understanding Sustainability: This chapter delved into the foundational principles of sustainability that underpin green entrepreneurship, highlighting the three pillars of economic, environmental, and social responsibility.

3. Launching Your Green Entrepreneurial Venture: We provided a roadmap for aspiring green entrepreneurs, from ideation and business planning to financing and legal considerations.

4. Scaling and Growing Your Green Business: Chapter 4 focused on expanding your green venture, discussing product diversification, marketing strategies, and financing for growth.

5. Sustaining Long-Term Success: We explored strategies for maintaining resilience, adaptability, and a strong commitment to sustainability as your business matures.

6. The Future of Green Entrepreneurship: Chapter 6 looked ahead to emerging trends and opportunities in green entrepreneurship, from clean energy to circular business models.

7. The Legacy of Green Entrepreneurship: We discussed the legacy you can leave as a green entrepreneur, from long-term thinking to mentorship and impact assessment.

8. Resources and Further Reading: Chapter 8 provided a curated list of books, online resources, organizations, and tools to support green entrepreneurs in their ongoing journey.

9. Your Personal Journey in Green Entrepreneurship: In this chapter, we explored the personal aspects of your journey, from self-care to ethical leadership and values-driven entrepreneurship.

10. Fostering a Sustainable Legacy and Continuous Impact: We highlighted the importance of long-term thinking, mentorship, and impact assessment in leaving a lasting legacy in green entrepreneurship.

11. Challenges and Future Considerations: Chapter 11 delved into ongoing challenges and emerging trends, including economic uncertainties, regulatory changes, and opportunities in technology and consumer behavior.

12. The Global Impact of Green Entrepreneurship: In the final chapter, we discussed how green entrepreneurs contribute to global sustainability efforts, influence policy, and inspire change.

Throughout the book, we emphasized the role of green entrepreneurs in addressing pressing environmental and social challenges, influencing policy, inspiring change, and leaving a lasting legacy. Their work extends far beyond the business realm, contributing to a more sustainable and equitable future on a global scale.